Psychological Corporations

Psychological Corporations

Garrett Kalleberg

SPUYTENDUYVIL

New York City

ISBN 1-881471-84-5

Spuyten Duyvil
PO Box 1852
Cathedral Station
New York, NY 10025
http://www.spuytenduyvil.net

Acknowledgements

"The Garden" appeared in *Global City Review*, Fall 1993.
"Agoraphobia" appeared in *American Letters & Commentary*,
Spring 1996. "The Last Seven" appeared in *Sulfur*, Fall 1996.
"House Tree Person Test" appeared in *Mandorla*, Winter 1997.
"In Neat and Orderly Rows" appeared in *First Intensity*, Winter
1997. "When I Was a Child" appeared in *American Letters &
Commentary*, Spring 1998. "The New Gate," and "Inside-the-
Body-Test" appeared in *An Anthology of New (American) Poets*,
Talisman House Publishers, 1998. Thanks to the editors of
these publications, and special thanks to Walter Sipser, Heather
Ramsdell, Laird Hunt, and Rebecca Tuggle.

Psychological Corporations was winner of the 1999 Poetry New
York Pamphlet Series.

Contents

I. Individual Examples

From a Psychological Atlas

Look at this picture then describe it
as areas of the body at which
whatever is sensed is vibration
during singing, tell me

do you feel it do you
feel it here or here and now
what does it feel like does it
feel real good to you?

Look at this picture.
As areas are pointed out at which
a chair & a chair is sensed
across from the chair & the body

is sitting vibrating at
very very small scale small
pitch as of microscopic
singing tell me

what does it feel like does it
feel good does it feel real?

Agoraphobia

In the allegory of the crowd horror
has an exhilarating effect—one-way streets
leading on to one-way streets of
shadow, where the redundant looks of the other
in situation, troubled, in flesh
& un-homelike
harbor images of the
bearded men top hats small black notebooks.
There's no escaping analysis.
But why not try?
On this day in July we could further ask
what is the nature of this wish, the ship
where greatness & indolence meet in the night, because
he was sipping wine in the late sun and his head
was beginning to ache,
because he did not have any convictions, the hero
with the broken arms
or bad luck, rotten credit, whereas he knew that
he didn't want the sun he wanted a complete and total stranger,
cigarettes, he wanted
solitude, gas lights, in black & white, a seat
at the panorama and the whole
glorious diorama of pedestrians going around, very slowly,
for walks.

Not rats.

        "Are they not all human beings?"
        Are they not all human beings,—
unique individuals in flesh, private souls out
for a quiet stroll, unmoored for the moment from daily routine
and passing to & fro by no
opportunities. Are they not all typical
in their way, the man in the velvet frock coat having troubled

to obtain a truly exceptional Pauillac
to be sipped on the sofa while the sun goes down.
Are they not all not unlike yourself, after having analyzed
the various possibilities,
not unlike the vision of the poet
on the sofa, not exactly heroic and yet
in situation not at all undesirable, black notebook cozy in his lap,
nor perhaps even unattainable, having finally
seen his way home down
the right one way street, shadows adrift in a
sea of Arcades, Social Movement, Dreams of the Future,
Conspiracies, Ruin
of Paris in which there is no other
reply, before it is late now, head beginning to ache, before it is
fear, fear now of going outside, going
around, very slowly,
for walks.

Not rats.

Dark

And now: the electrical stimulation of a frog

And now: the electric light bulb

And now: the electrocution of an elephant

And now, ladies and gentleman in the dark: the dark.

The room is dark, madness

is dark, comedy is dark, the night is dark
when the curtains are closed shutting
out the street
light, I have dark thoughts these nights, dreams
which are pretty violent, I
hope this doesn't mean anything I've
never hurt a thing, really, not including
when Bryan and I went crazy with a
BB gun upstate, we were young, children
can be cruel, children are cruel.

Inside-of-the-Body Test

There will be one point for a correct answer
no point for no answer
and minus one point for every lie.
You will have five seconds to respond
five milliseconds
nanoseconds
revolutions of an electron
in a hydrogen atom
of a drop of water
in the vitreous humor of your right eye—
What's inside you, man? what's
keeping you alive! or is the question
too difficult, the eye
convoluted so
inward, on the repetition of one act
in the memory's
screen and all the individual
scenes become one   one
          cause
                    which is the *real* cause,
heart   liver   spine   bowels   blood—
I must make a confession.
The senses bound to follow an inner
command, which is its own reward
even as certain thoughts attach themselves
to this image   tries to get out
and a muscle flinches
I could hit myself.

The Garden

The sun is low & the room is empty.
Not any room but your room.
You sit in your room which is empty, and
you imagine it to be empty. Which it is not.

A daydream fills your mind, a novel
& agreeable passion, perhaps you are not quite happy
in your room. Perhaps you would like
a beaver hat, peppercorns, fine silk, gunpowder—

black tea, cardamom—deerskin, sugar—
a new sealskin for the ballroom—a new
chart for the map room—a new philosophy
for the bedroom—a new Venus for the garden—

"Chase the Vices from the Garden."
One cultivates one's own garden. The garden
is out the window—it is not
your garden. The garden

is empty. It's winter.
Winter is empty, it's spring.

Late spring or summer and
the sun is low and the window is closed

and the air conditioner is on
and all of life

is buzzing around your head.
Your life. No need to go to sea.

House Tree Person Test

Sometimes at night I can hear you saying,
Take this, eat; drink this
and don't forget me—is this the test?
Is this the order. Another idea recollects me.
Sometimes I listen, and hear the sea.
Word by word. Vast, waste. Sea of boat

lost on the sea.
Mazy & shifting, these lanes of internecine,
and the transference is in place—
no matter what the clouds portend
no matter how auspicious the winding
to & fro, back & forth, up & down in the whorl between the devil
and the deep blue sea, What good is a leaky boat
on a sea of flames? What good is a skiff
on the lake of fire?
Which illuminates another problem.

Timor mortis pertvrbat me become
tendency, timidity, trait:
The seed is in the earth
as its fruit, the tree is in the seed
as its fruit, the boat
is in the tree as its fruit.
Now I have killed the tree, root, egregious

indexical. And at night, I can hear the fire
that consumes all things—Death
is in the fear of death as the fruit
of fear—"what are *you* doing here?
You ought to go photograph the fire too."

Here I have something for you.
Tintypes, 10¢.

17

Here's a bit of something for you.
Tintypes, 10¢.

You will be a tintypist of ecstatic effects.
You will make a good ashtray.
You will make a good critic, moving in
amongst the ashes, there is an extra room
in the north side of the house.

Take this, it's the most comfortable chair
in the house. In several minutes you will be my guest, ecstatic
guest for what effect—is it better to be still
or move a lot? the earth moves, the sun
moves, the universe moves in a disconcerting way,

there is a mover.
Take this. In my house are two mansions, and
in this mansion are two rooms and
in this room is a small and quiet room. And

from this room is another room and
from this room is another room and...
a chair. This is a chair with electrical contacts
in the seat and arms this measures
movements and is almost always undetected
by subjects even if subjects knew that
they were being measured, it is hard to fake.
Is it better to be still or move a lot?
Cheating can easily be detected, this is the line
between seven types of personality

for which we have a simple test.
Draw a line as slowly as possible.
This is the line, it's chalk.
This is chalk, it's sand.
Sand says,

"you are hungry, thirsty, arguing
for the infinite particularity of
shifting about into sand"

and the sand turned into the sea.
Into the sea tread the boat of flames.
Into *the devil to pay and
no pitch hot.*
It is hard to fake hot pitch.

Forces Act Upon the Skin

I sped towards a lake in
upstate New York where I laid
in the grass and thought,
let the rest of the world catch up with me.
Likewise a touch, a caress, thoughtful
and attentive, moves at times
towards a sudden withdrawal—a
heightening of intensity, of feeling or
depth, reaching down into the very innermost,

it's a long way down.
Sound of slow slide whistle.
Wind in the thistle.
Crickets. Cow bells.

How beautiful it is here, that I
want to get out of my own skin, take a walk
before dinner, up the mountain,
Mont Blanc rosy pink now glowing
in the distance.
DEFENSE ABSOLUE
DANGER DE MORT, written across

an electrical tower—in this world
electromagnetic forces are
stronger than gravity, I know
but how I've always wanted

to fly—there was a boy
in Staten Island climbed an electrical
pole, one summer and
touched the wire, the shock
stopped his heart—he was dead—falling
to the ground, when the force of
hitting the street started

his heart again, he

walked home, complained
of some pain, took off
his clothes and with it
his skin.

If We Are in the Air, Make a Bang

If we are in the air, don't check for no fall.
If we are dead, don't check for killability.
If we just got hit, put out some smoke.
If we are dead, take shallow breaths

through a cloth or small towel.
Consider the time if should take to evacuate.
Consider the weather, the time of day.

What to do before.
What to do during.
What to do after.

Shortly after 8 p.m., missiles started to fall

like rains on Prishtina. Some five of them were seen

and they were furtive
like flames and falling

like stars. Perhaps
those
watching from the windows felt the rush

of the wind blow on their nose and chest. A big smoke and fire
on the western side of Prishtina.

The Individual Example

if there were an infinity of infinitely unhappy life to be won. But
here there is an infinity of infinitely unhappy life to be won, and
won and won and won from the pinnacle
of the pyramid to the cupola
of the bell curve, bellowing
of the ancient mob mass crowd in Paris
in the nineteenth century—Why don't the
people people legs
walking left add legs
walking right subtract the individual
surviving in numbers, human
aggregate. And for every one of them exists
a simpler term, the nonconformist negative, lilting

by way of the seven bridges of Königsberg,
it is impossible to avoid repetition.
It is impossible to avoid the line.
Never mind the moral questions:
It is impossible to stay where you are without going
backwards STEP
FORWARD AND STATE
YOUR BUSINESS
say Yes. One door says Yes, the other door
says No. Keep closed. Keep a faithful

watch and wait, the rest will follow.
There is another train behind this one:
all explained in the law of theoretical
distribution—Are you with me? I'm going
in there, a very clear action for a night action.
Now I get to give you a couple of hugs

before I turn my back on you again, Good night.
And now I'm going and never coming back.
And she stormed off up into the attic and waited for me

like the time she stormed off up into the attic
and waited for me, later we talked about it, she said
she wanted me to come up and say
Doctor? an honor and a pleasure you yourself admit

was. Never mind the historical questions: we were made
to go this way and that and all along
remember the details
it is impossible to forget, maybe
that's the way out—try the gate, but
don't answer the phone.
Where'd they get your number?
Somewhere there's a list
kept in a book and
Answer the phone!—if not, they will
say *he* was
and *she* was and they
were used, these are the details.

As It Is

She is the one lying in bed.
He is the one lying in bed.
They are the ones that do
anything you tell them to.
His hand pressed hard against her mouth
until she stopped screaming—

it's funny how we both came
to this, that we had lost our charm.
Now I will make them sleep
a very deep sleep.
Was he dead? (this is the second dream).
Was it an accident? (this was the first dream).

The world is
as it is
I said. Human in almost
every abstract
the least of these being love

you

you are crying

II. The Last Seven

When I Was a Child

When I was a child I spoke
as a child, I understood
as a child, I thought
as a child; I
had a wooden reel with a piece of string
tied to it; I held the reel
by the piece of string
tied to it, and skillfully threw it
over the edge of my curtained cot
so that it disappeared into it.
O O O O O
I said, and hailed its reappearance
with a joyful "da,"
there. There, the interpretation of the game
is obvious disappearance and return
of the object at hand.
There,
so that it was gone
into it—alright
go away then,
I've had my revenge.
I write these things
being absent
lest being present I
use harsher words.

Hollow Chamber

And once out

And once we walked
out of waking, expectation

And once we tried to run but
could not get out.

Once out of the suffocating air
of that room

into bright crisp reeds
dryly whispering
at the southeastern edge of the sea—

Dumb.

Dumb as a hollow reed, rising
out of the sea.
I say nothing—Say nothing

that cannot be said.
The wind is dry.
The sound, hollow. The sound

dead in this hall, in this chamber, channel,
or shaft—the sound

is as tall and wide as a small child—cut
out of the sunny mountainside.

In Neat & Orderly Rows

Zazetsky was in the crouching position, and next to him
the jawbone of a boar.
Here find a philosophical fragment
of redeemable purposiveness, supposing truth
and presence coincide.

Zazetsky was in the crouching position, and on his breast
were the antlers of a stag.
A piece of an antler anyway.
And that is enough for purposiveness
and truth to coincide.

Like a parergon of several words arranged
quite plausibly and
on a page for starters where you know
almost every word you see, except for Vereinigungspunkt
and parergon
which you can look up if you like and do
but something about this particular order, doesn't
quite ring a bell.
You can go ask the philosopher's stone,
go ask the philosopher's tree, go
ask the philosopher's
table & chair, here & now,—

What's in the bag?

It's Nothing.

Otherwise it wouldn't be
a philosopher's bag.

I open my bag and pull out a stove a smoke a
chimney a fire a torch a candle a house a flame
a light a cat, cast iron.

I open my book and pull out a word a line a frame
around the sky above the ground below the trees in
neat and orderly rows,—

It's the hour after, time to work the field.

With a scythe, for cutting. With a hoe, for turning
over the earth. With a shovel for digging...

It is the day after, time has well worked this field.

With a shovel for shovelling. With a brush
for brushing. With a bag. A
string for making a grid, it looks like. With
a ruler for comparison, a pencil and notebook
for writing, for taking notes—so we find ourselves

reading the events of the day in a comfortable
room on the eighth floor. At last
we have conquered our baser selves
and quite plausibly, having
made use of the latest techniques and lack
of sentiment, uncovering what came first, what we are,
and where, though

closer digging reveal the mind
divided into two compartments, chambers or
barely livable cells:
first, containing the mindless
beast from which we evolved;
the second, containing the night watchman,
least of which we evolved

and a salami sandwich for food.
And next to that a piece of rope
for tying, a video camera

for viewing, a can of Pepsi
or Coke, a note—

It is the day after.
Who reveals the face in the stream
or in the wood
floor boards on the floor
covering up the underfloor, the hollow
ground, the clean and secret chamber
or cell?

Two days later he was found
in the crouching position:
his feet in the earth, his mouth in the dust.

Which Is the Whole

for Heather

And the sea did not move
and I did not move
and that was the pattern

in a curve that reaches
almost immediately
to infinity (either positive

or negative) linked
rings carved of boxwood

do not separate
do not come undone

or the lesson is sad
they must be
broken, or one

must be, to show you
which is the whole
lesson, the pattern.

The New Gate

    to bind

    to keep

    to separate

    to take in
like a gate, opening to concrete
fields, streams, states. At the edge

not shadow, not light—
forms moving, at the periphery forms

waiting. By the wall,
figures marching—in dark blue
or black—it is dark, too dark

to tell. It is hard to tell
one from another, gray
forms blocked out against a gray field,
as when one looks at a photograph
or map, a plan reproduced
in the newspapers—I seem to have
lost the clipping—what is ever left
anyway? The wall may be razed,
the plan remains.
The gate may be destroyed,

there will be a better gate
to stand the test—against which
all people move, though they may not know
where they're going.

Without obstacle,
the train pulls in—time

35

can be told by it—the new train
enters the gate,

but it does not go out again.
Following a straight line, bodies
enter in at the periphery.
But they do not go out again.

One could see, it is a good wall
and a good gate, opening

to a steady stream of gray figures,—nothing
is ever lost. Nothing has ever lived

and is lost to the mind which can

     receive

     divide

     hold

     bind,
as certainly as a concrete wall, a gate
or station—a state of rest
by a field of dead grasses.

Agent and Reagent

The rules do not apply to you but you
and I have run out of time.

Funny, I always know how this will end
then write a new beginning. And it all works
like clock work.
Next line:

Open new window with message / dialog / alert:
is it safe?

A visitor visits.

A receiver receives.

An agent will be right with you.

I was a tool, said Eichmann, *in the hands of superior powers
and authorities*—damn, upstairs the landlord
is beating his wife again—or yelling at her, don't
exaggerate, but that crash, at 5 o'clock one morning and those
sounds, of her crying? *I am not stupid,*
he says, *I know what you are doing down here, why
do you have so many boxes?* and his routine about
where the garbage cans that they are placed
just so, there are rules, the Law
makes sin, said Paul.

Is it safe? Are you safe there, even my brother

and my sister, whom I love so, increasingly
perfect beings becoming increasingly
aware of increasingly
imperfect time.

Perfect that those lines
get shorter—now what? begin again? I should
open a window, get some
fresh—who am I talking to? and who
sent me the message:

DO NOT INTERRUPT DELIVERY TO RECEIVER.

I should explain.

That at exactly 12:10 AM a photograph will be taken of my garbage
can from 5 miles up and in 2 or 3 years I could buy it for cheap.

That exactly 12:30 AM a
photograph etc. There's an advertisement in *Wired*.

That in this state the system exists for itself, and it all works
like clock work.

That *The formula that describes the state of the self when despair
is completely rooted out is this: in relating itself to itself and in willing
to be itself, the self rests transparently in the power that established it.*
Which is *The Sickness Unto Death*:

That the failure was in the wrong system and disconnected it.

Wait a minute. Wait a minute.
I'm getting something in:
All agents are busy.

A satellite on the horizon, lost
packets in the pipeline. A
momentary surge, the kitchen light, a grid
rises, falls. The receiver is dead,
Brother:

an alarm clock rings in the evidence locker.

Traceroute, Carrier

An action requiring a connection was requested
when there was no connection

An unexpected error with no useful information
has occurred

A flash of light, percussive bolt
and something presses his hand

> against the air
> until the air gives way and
> part of him has made it across

and part a neural net
holds. Until commanded

to be thrown:

until an outer limit is reached and the whole
implodes in a sharp blow
to the back of the head—can we all live
eternally in such marvellous ecstasy
or in such ecstatic mystery

and at this frequency?
bits of initially co-moving particles
in free fall.

A particle confined to a domain whose dimensions
are of the order of the wavelength of the particle,

and at this frequency, shift
to red, angels radiating from the sun
precisely along the line of sight of the observer

(so that they are never actually seen:

matter with high angular momentum
attracted to Being

does not
fall directly into Being

                  but forms a rapidly spinning

        flash of light

and something presses his hand.
He sits at the table in the dark
He sits at the table

and one speaks, carries the signal
and another waits until one has stopped
has ceased speaking
All the other guests must wait
until carrier ceases
before trying to transmit
One speaks
another waits
in order to speak
All others must wait
in the dark, until carrier ceases
The guests sit at the table
in carrier sense
One ceases speaking.

The Last Seven

[And] had in his right hand stars
The mystery of the stars
and the golden candlesticks
The stars are the angels of the
angels of the churches
the candlesticks which thou
thou sawest are the churches
holdeth the stars in his right hand
of the golden candlesticks
hath the Spirits of God
and the stars
were lamps of fire burning
are the Spirits of God. And before the throne
sealed with seals
and to loose the seals thereof?
as it had been slain, having horns
horns and eyes, which are
are the Spirits of God
saw the angels which stood
and to them were given
the angels which had the
thunders uttered their voices
when the thunders had uttered
which the thunders uttered, and write
slain of men thousand: and the remnant
having heads
horns, and crowns upon his heads
up out of the sea, having heads
angels having the last
angels come out of the
temple, having the plagues, clothed in
beasts gave unto the angels
the plagues of the angels
voice out of the temple saying to the angels
and the angel poured out

of the angels
which had the vials
of blasphemy, having heads
that carrieth her, which hath the heads
The heads are mountains
And there are kings

[And] he is the eighth, and is of the
the angels which had the
vials full
of the seven last plagues, and
                              talked with me

Garrett Kalleberg's *Limbic Odes* was published by Heart Hammer in 1997. His poetry has appeared in various journals, including *Sulfur, First Intensity, Talisman, Denver Quarterly, Mandorla,* and *American Letters & Commentary,* and in *An Anthology of New (American) Poets* (Talisman House, 1998). His awards for poetry and critical writing include two awards from the Academy of American Poets and a grant from Poets & Writers. He edits and publishes the online poetry & criticism journal *The Transcendental Friend,* and the text-based audio CD imprint Immanent Audio.